Gwenllian F
The Warrior Prii

By Laurel A. Rockefeller

Cover art derived from the Codex Manasse, 1304.
Music excerpted from the "Pais Dinogad" (7th century).

This book is work of narrative history based on events in the life of Princess Gwenllian ferch Gruffydd ap Cynan and constructed using primary and secondary historical sources, commentary, and research.

Consulted sources appear at the end of this book. Interpretation of source material is at the author's discretion and utilized within the scope of the author's imagination, including names, events, and historical details.

Copyright © 2016 Laurel A. Rockefeller
Published by Laurel A. Rockefeller Books.
Johnstown, Pennsylvania. USA
All rights reserved.
ISBN: 1533365776
ISBN-13: 978-1533365774

Share the love of this book and the Legendary Women of World History Series by kindly reviewing this book on your blog, website, and on major retailer websites. Your review not only offers this author your feedback for improvement of this book series, but helps other people find this book so they can enjoy it as well. Only a few sentences and a few minutes of your time is all it takes to share the love with those who want to enjoy it too.

Check out these related biographies from the Legendary Women of World History Series

Empress Matilda of England

Queen Elizabeth Tudor: Journey to Gloriana

Mary Queen of the Scots, the Forgotten Reign

TABLE OF CONTENTS

"GWENLLIAN'S TEARS" 5

CHAPTER ONE 6

CHAPTER TWO 9

CHAPTER THREE 15

CHAPTER FOUR... 22

CHAPTER FIVE 27

TIMELINE 35

SUGGEST READING AND BIBLIOGRAPHY 44

ABOUT THIS SERIES.. 53

"Gwenllian's Tears"

Cry out for me, my people.
Where my blood was spilt, let your voices be heard
forever more.
Cymru in all your glory:
Deheubarth, Gwynedd, Ceredigion, Powys, Dyfed
Ynys Môn where I was born!
Let not these conquerors go unanswered
Swear to me you shall never forget.
We are Cymraeg.
We are forever.

Chapter One

"The king welcomes into his court Princess Nest ferch Rhys of Deheubarth, baroness of Pembroke!" cried the herald as she processed through the great hall of King Gruffydd ap Cynan's castle in Aberffraw on the coast of Ynys Môn in the northwest of Gruffydd's kingdom.

Confidently the twenty nine year old princess strode to greet King Gruffydd and kneeled respectfully at the king on his throne, "Bore da, f'arglwydd."

"Bore da f'arglwyddes," smiled Gruffydd as he motioned for her to rise. "Sut ydych chi?

"Da iawn, diolch yn fawr. My son Henry Fitzhenry gives his kind regards."

King Gruffydd rose and stepped down from the dais. Nodding, he motioned for her to follow him, "Your husband does not mind he is King Henry's son?"

"Gerald of Windsor is the king's man, a baron because King Henry wants him watching over the marches and keeping we Welsh firmly under *his* control. Henry Fitzhenry is with his stepfather right now in Cernarth along with our children."

"Has he grown much since I last saw him?"

"He's almost ten now," replied Nest simply with a smile.

"Tell me my lady, are you here just to visit with old friends or does other business occupy your mind?"

"By business do you mean the king's business or my own?"

"Is there a difference?" questioned King Gruffydd shrewdly.

"In this case yes; if King Henry were to find out about this errand up north he would be more than a little cross with me, despite his fond memories of me from his youth," admitted Nest.

"What could you say or do to make our liege lord cross?"

"I have a favour to ask you."

"A favour? How expensive a favour?"

"My brother Hywel has healed from the injuries he suffered while imprisoned by Arnulf fitz Roger of Montgomery. I've kept him with me in Pembroke, but it grows dangerous for me to harbour him. No one has any idea what happened to my brother Llewelyn and—"Nest fell suddenly silent, much to King Gruffydd's alarm.

"What doom do you bring to my kingdom, Nest? What are you trying not to tell me?"

"My brother Gruffydd ap Rhys has returned from his exile in Ireland. In the few months he's stayed with me he has already been proclaimed a champion by the people eager for us to throw off this pretend vassalage towards King Henry of England. They would see him crowned king of Deheubarth as our father's heir and rightful ruler of our lands. King Henry wants him dead."

"The Normans always went us dead, or at very least subservient," observed King Gruffydd.

"Not all Normans," flirted Nest. "I find my husband agreeable enough, not to mention a certain king of England whose bed I shared for many years—even after he married the noble Princess Matilda of Scotland, daughter of Saint Margaret of Wessex. Quite the pedigree but I am more beautiful, more to his *liking*. You wouldn't care to find out personally now would you?"

Gruffydd looked at her, partly with a man's eye for beauty and partly with a king's eye for politics, "You are beautiful, Nest."

"Does that mean I should expect you in my room tonight?" smiled Nest as she put her arms around his neck and kissed him.

"Why do you want me right now?"

"You are a king; my husband has no noble blood at all. I married him because my Henry needed me to bear his bastard away from court and the disproving eyes of Queen Matilda. My son and his daughter Matilda are almost the same age, you know."

"Conceived no doubt while the queen was pregnant with her daughter."

"How did you know?"

"I am a king—and a man."

"So that does that mean you accept my offer?"

"No, Nest, not that one. But I will receive your brothers here in Aberffraw and give them sanctuary if they need it. I value Deheubarth far too much as an ally to risk it on some *whim* of yours."

Nest released him from her embrace, "A pity. You would have found tonight quite entertaining had you accepted."

Gruffydd stepped away from her, "Entertaining perhaps. But what good is a night of entertainment if it undermines my kingdom? Sleeping with you might have its benefits, Nest, but not nearly the benefits I seek from strengthening my alliance with Deheubarth. Your brother Gruffydd is your father's heir. He is far more valuable to me in freeing our people from the Normans and the English than you will ever be!"

Chapter Two

Several weeks later two heavily cloaked and hooded men rode silently to the gates of Aberffraw Castle, its wind polished stones wet with light rain. As the horses gently cantered into the centre courtyard a mother duck quacked to the five young ducklings following her. A rooster crowed to his hens as he strutted near the horses. A groom met the men and held the reins for them as they dismounted before leading the tired and hungry horses to King Gruffydd ap Cynan's stables. Pulling the hoods off their faces the young men finally relaxed. They were safe at last.

"Noswaith dda, f'arglwydd," bowed Prince Gruffydd Ap Rhys, his short brown hair still damp from the bath he and his brother Hywel took upon their arrival.

King Gruffydd smiled at the young men, "Noswaith dda! I am glad to see you safe in my castle at last."

Prince Hywel bowed to the king, "We are most grateful for your protection, my lord."

"Your father was a good friend, Hywel. He was noble and kind. He loved this land and loved freedom as a prince of Wales ought to," affirmed King Gruffydd.

"We are most grateful you were able to continue resisting King William Rufus' invasions in our absence," added Prince Gruffydd.

"We are neighbours, Deheubarth and Gwynedd. We must work together to remain free."

"Team work is not in our blood, my lord. Though it cost us our freedom it has never been our strength. Even at the height of our liberty –before the Romans came and massacred the druid teachers—we could not manage to put aside our differences for the common defence of our lands. Is not this castle built where the legends say the druids fought to keep us free?" asked Prince Gruffydd.

"If not this spot, then very near," confirmed King Gruffydd. "Sometimes we find something—a bowl, a cup, a pitcher—from that time."

"I am not saying that unity is easy for us; only that we must work together. To that aim I will do anything within my power to help you."

Hywel shuffled closer to the king, the agony of his injuries flashing across his face against his will, "You are not afraid of King Henry?"

King Gruffydd picked up his cup and motioned for a steward to hand Prince Gruffydd and Prince Hywel cups of wine, "I am of three royal houses; I fear only slavery. Death in battle is nothing to me, as long as I die with honour like your father." The king raised his cup high, "To King Rhys ap Tewdr! God rest his soul!"

"GOD REST HIS SOUL," echoed the sons of King Rhys.

That night Hywel came to his brother's chamber as both readied for bed, a small lamp in his hand, "Gruffydd, do you really think we can trust this king of Gwynedd to keep us safe from the English?"

"Our father trusted him. We trusted him while he lived."

"That was before the English killed Gronwy in prison and before they tortured and maimed me. I may never recover from these wounds, Gruffydd."

Gruffydd poured himself a cup of water and took a sip, "I know. I wish I could do more to help your agony."

"I am a prince of Deheubarth; I can manage."

"So you are," agreed Gruffydd.

"Did you hear the gossip from the servants?"

"What gossip?"

"They say our sister tried on King Gruffydd what she used to do with the English king—only Gruffydd rebuffed her and turned her away."

"Nest is her own woman."

"But must she behave so disgracefully?"

"Hywel, surely you understand that neither the Normans nor the English honour and respect women like we Welsh do. Their common law is different than our common law; it's more patriarchal; women have fewer rights among the English than they do among us. Nest is using the tools she possesses. In her own way, she is fighting them too."

"Four years as King Henry's mistress hardly seems like fighting the English," scoffed Hywel.

"To survive Nest must tread very carefully Hywel. Would you prefer she die at English hands?"

"An honourable princess of Deheubarth would do nothing less, Gruffydd."

"Yes—death is easy. Cooperation is far more difficult. It does not matter if the compromise is with a friend or a foe. We always prefer to die."

Three nights later Prince Gruffydd found himself unable to sleep. Dressing himself in the dark he put on his warmest cloak and headed into the main courtyard for some fresh air.

The sky above him glistened with stars that seemed especially bright after the storm that greeted him before. In the starlight stood a lady with red hair neatly braided down her back and covered only with a simple circlet. Gruffydd approached her, "Noswaith dda, f'arglwyddes."

The lady turned to him, "Noswaith dda, f'arglwydd."

"You do not cover your hair like most ladies do," observed Gruffydd.

"Cymraes ydw i. I have no need for English fashions."

"They say even the great ladies in Scotland wear the veil."

"The nobles of Scotland care more about money than they do honour. The Normans bought them. You cannot buy me."

"Spoken like a true lady of this land," smiled Gruffydd.

"Aberffraw is my home. I need no other."

"Well said, f'arglwyddes." Gruffydd took a step closer to her, "May I beg your indulgence and inquire of your name?"

"Gwenllian ydw i," she smiled. "Gwenllian ferch Gruffydd ap Cynan."

Gruffydd fell to his knees, "F'arglwyddes!"

"Gruffydd ap Rhys ydych chi?" asked Gwenllian.

"Ydw. How long have you known my name, Your Highness?"

"It is not hard to guess who you are, Gruffydd. And since your brother's gait is impaired by his injuries it is only logical that you would be the heir to Rhys ap Tewder's throne."

"The English are a cruel enemy to fight," affirmed Gruffydd.

"Do you think I know nothing of warfare? My mother is a daughter of the king of Dublin. My father has fought his entire life to free Gwynedd from English control. Do you think only my brother Owain studies the arts of war? Nay, my lord. I am Welsh, not some Norman lady who lives to breed at her father and husband's pleasure. When it is time for me to marry it shall be of my own choosing!"

"Of that I have no doubt, Your Highness."

"Why do you call me that?"

"Why not? You are a princess and if I may be so bold, a very beautiful young woman."

"Perhaps it is the starlight. Perhaps in the light of day you will think otherwise."

"I am willing to find out. Are you willing to let me see you by daylight?"

"Before or after you touch me as King Henry touched your sister?" asked Gwenllian astutely.

"I swear to you my lady I shall not touch you in such a manner short of binding myself to you in accord with the laws and customs of this land."

"So be it then," agreed Gwenllian as she turned to return inside.

"May I see you another time? By daylight or starlight or candle? I care not how I see you, my lady. Please, I ask you, may I see you again?"

"You are our guest. If it pleases you for me to join you when you dine, you need only ask my father and I will come."

Chapter Three

The next evening Princess Gwenllian glided down the stairs into her father's banqueting hall in a pale blue gown edged with embroidered white roses and yellow daffodils. Seated next to King Gruffydd in a place of honour Prince Gruffydd smiled at her, his eyes widened with appreciation for both the beauty of the princess and her choice of gown. The prince turned to the king, "Might I ask a favour of you, f'arglwydd? Please kindly permit your daughter to dine in the seat next mine?"

King Gruffydd looked at him keenly, "You have already become acquainted?"

"Not by candlelight, no. Only by starlight!" replied Prince Gruffydd distantly, his thoughts fixated upon the princess.

Princess Gwenllian reached her father and hugged him warmly. The king kissed her cheek, "Do you know this man, Gwenllian?"

"I am still a maid if that is what you are asking," teased Gwenllian. Straightening up she looked her father in the eye, "We spoke briefly in the courtyard. I was studying the stars and our guest came out in pursuit of fresh air to calm restless limbs."

King Gruffydd nodded, "You may dine next to him if you desire."

Smiling Gwenllian sat in the empty seat next to the prince. Prince Gruffydd turned to her quietly, "You look beautiful tonight, Your Highness. Did you wear this gown to please me? I could not help but to notice the cenhinen pedr embroidered among the roses. A most beautiful flower. Oh but to show you the cenhinen pedr in Ceredigion! There is one special field I know in Aberystwyth where they bloom like a carpet of gold. The ladies of Aberystwyth have taken to wearing them in their hair on Saint David's Day. Did you know that?"

"Saint David was born in Ceredigion was he not?"

"Yes. The leek is his symbol. Legend has it he bade those fighting for Welsh freedom against the Saxons to mark their allegiance by wearing a leek in their hats."

"What is Ceredigion like?"

"It is on the shores of the Irish sea. It rains a great deal. In Aberystwyth the stormy tide sometimes reaches higher than the walls around your castle. It is best to not be too close to the beach when the weather storms like that," laughed Prince Gruffydd playfully.

"The storms get pretty bad here too sometimes, especially with one wall of the castle on the cliff above the sea," agreed Gwenllian.

From across the table Prince Hywel eyed his brother, "What are you two whispering about, Gruffydd?"

Prince Gruffydd turned his attention to Hywel, "The weather if you must know."

"The weather?" asked Hywel incredulously. "Why would you whisper about the weather?" Princess Gwenllian looked at Hywel. Infectious laughter burst from her heart. Prince Gruffydd joined her. Queen Angharad shook her head gaily as the entire table, including the king's oldest son Prince Owain, fell into mirth.

Saint David's Day arrived to warmth and sunshine. In her room Princess Gwenllian sat next to the window on a stool, her fingers playing a folk song on her Welsh harp as she sang, "Pan elai dy dad di i'r mynydd. Deuai ef ag un iwrch, un twrch coed, un hydd." Prince Gruffydd knocked on the door and then entered. Gwenllian continued the song on her harp, "Un rugiar fraith o fynydd, a physgodyn o readr Derwennydd. Beth bynnag a gyrhaeddai dy dad â'i bicell -Boed yn dwrch, yn gath goed, yn lwynog -Ni ddihangai'r un oni bai'n nerthol ei adenydd."

"Don't stop, my lady. You sing and play so beautifully," smiled Prince Gruffydd.

"That is all of the song I know—just the end of it."

"Do you know the songs of your mother's people in Dublin?"

"Only on the harp."

"Will you play something from Ireland for me? I was in exile in Ireland for most of these last few years you know. I will never forget how beautiful the music was. So many evenings near the fire and letting the music fill my soul!"

Gwenllian began to play, "I cannot sing or play as well as my father's court bard."

"Why would I want to listen to him when your company is so much fairer and you are so much more beautiful?" flirted the prince softly. Gwenllian rose from her harp and sat down on the edge of her bed. Gruffydd sat down beside her, "Tell me something, Your Highness: would I be over reaching my station in life if I kissed you, a mere prince of Deheubarth?" Gwenllian shook her head shyly. Slowly, tenderly the prince kissed her.

Princess Gwenllian savoured the kiss before looking him in the eyes, "How many others have there been? How many conquests have you made?"

"I am a poor prince, Your Highness. I do not dare chance the fine for inflicting a child upon a mistress nor the other fines that such dalliances provoke, not again anyway. There was once a girl in Ireland who captured my imagination. We had two sons together, Anarawd and Cadell. I do not know what happened to them—or their mother."

"Do you still love her?" asked Gwenllian shyly, uncertain if she wanted her question answered.

"My sons, yes. I am natural man after all. But their mother? I look at that time in my life and I wonder what possessed me to be with her." Sensing Gwenllian's discomfort he took her hand gently, "Do not be afraid, my lady! No contract binds me to anyone. The past is the past. I do not love her. I do not want her. I want your love and none other."

"Because I am the king's daughter? Is that why you desire me now? Am I a path to power for you?"

Gruffydd kissed her tenderly, "No, my lady!"

"Does that mean you would contract with me for my hand in marriage should I consent in heart, body, and soul to such a match?"

"If you and your father would consent to this, I think I would be most happy."

Gwenllian smiled at him shyly, "Let us not contemplate such things today. The weather is fair and I would so much like to practice with my bow and with my sword."

Gwenllian ferch Gruffydd, the Warrior Princess of Deheubarth

"Well then practice we shall! For Ceredigion, Deheubarth, and Saint David!" rejoiced Prince Gruffydd.

"Dydd Gŵyl Dewi Hapus!"

Prince Gruffydd and Princess Gwenllian played with practice swords in the courtyard, enjoying the sunshine on this especially clear day. Gruffydd was particularly pleased when Gwenllian defeated him; clearly they were evenly matched in battle prowess. As the sun reached mid-afternoon the king's servants set up archery targets. In a single line stood the king, the queen, Gwenllian, Prince Gruffydd, Prince Hywel, and Gwenllian's brother Owain in a friendly competition for the best score in which Gwenllian proved herself the equal to both her father and her suitor. As the sun began to set Prince Gruffydd gave the princess a daffodil. As she kissed him she felt a stirring in her heart. This man was her destiny. His people would become hers.

Several months later, in the year eleven fifteen Gwenllian's hope became reality. In a private wedding in the castle chapel she wed her prince at last, cementing in marriage the alliance between Gwynedd and Deheubarth and making both prince and princess the happiest of all men and women in Wales. Sons soon followed: Morgan, Maelgwn, Owain, Maredudd, and finally Rhys ap Gruffydd, forefather to England's Tudor dynasty thanks to the valour of Owain ap Maredudd ap Tudur and his love for the beautiful dowager queen Catherine de Valois. Happy and very much in love

Gwenllian and Gruffydd welcomed their twin daughters Nest and Gwladus in eleven thirty.

Across the years Gwenllian and Gruffydd struggled to keep their family together in face of what seemed like constant war with the Normans. From Pembroke Castle the Norman barons relentlessly battled with Gwenllian and Gruffydd for control of Deheubarth, often forcing them into the rugged Welsh mountains and away from their comfortable home in Dinefwr Castle.

In Gwynedd, Gwenllian's father Gruffydd ap Cynan grew older. No longer able to lead his armies in defence of Gwynedd himself, he delegated more and more responsibility for the safety and security of Gwynedd to her brothers Cadwallon, Owain Gwynedd, and Cadwaladr. Working together the brothers freed more and more lands south and east of Gwynedd from King Henry of England's control. The Deheubarth-Gwynedd alliance was working, freeing most of Wales from Anglo-Norman rule.

At home, King Henry of England had worse problems to deal with than the battle prowess of the children of King Gruffydd ap Cynan. In eleven twenty his only legitimate son with Queen Matilda of Scotland drowned in a terrible shipwreck off the coast of Normandy. With his surviving daughter Matilda safe in Germany and ruling as its empress, King Henry considered the succession secure. And why should it not be? Surely a legitimate daughter of his body was better heir than a nephew by his sister Adela of Normandy!

As the year eleven thirty five waned and King Henry sickened who could have imagined the treachery waiting to destroy not only the hopes and dreams of the king but those of every Welsh man, woman, and child over the next nine hundred years? After all, the king's daughter was in Anjou with her son Henry, far too far away to stop a grandson of William the Conqueror with dreams of seizing the throne for himself.

Chapter Four

Princess Gwenllian woke at dawn to the sound of alarm bells clanging furiously through Dinefwr Castle. Pulling back the curtains of her snug bed, she raced to put on a simple dress and belt, her servants all scattered in response to the bells. Buckling on her sword belt she slipped her feet into a pair of boots and ventured towards the courtyard where she spotted Gruffydd as he mounted his horse. "What news, Gruffydd? Why the alarm?"

"Carn Goch is under attack from the Normans!"

"What? On New Year's Day? Do not the English celebrate the holidays, especially with so much snow on the ground?"

"The English didn't start this one, my love; we did. I just received a report that over one thousand Welshman have marched up from the south to take back their farms and pastures from the Norman soldiers who displaced them. The people are cold and their flocks are starving. They are within their rights to take back their homes!"

Gwenllian motioned for the groom to prepare her horse and for another servant to fetch her cloak, "I couldn't agree more! That's why I'm coming with you!"

"You realize this could be a trap to capture us, don't you?" asked Gruffydd lovingly.

"It's always a trap, sweetheart!" laughed Gwenllian as one of her ladies pulled a heavy fur-lined cloak over her shoulders and fastened the clasp around her neck. Her groom brought out her now saddled horse, her bow and a quiver of arrows already packed in a saddlebag along with a fruitcake and a flask of mead brewed in the castle kitchens. Noticing the servants' expert preparations she smiled as she mounted her horse and rode out of the castle gate side by side with Gruffydd.

Gruffydd and Gwenllian did not need to travel far to find the battle. At just six miles distance Carn Goch was the nearest fortification to Dinefwr and a frequent royal home when Dinefwr itself ceased to be safe for their children. As the sturdy stones of the fortress came in view the prince and princess found a sea of bodies, nearly all of them Norman and most of them hacked beyond recognition. A few faint cries filled their ears from the wounded.

From the carnage a bloodied figure rode towards them on horseback, his face blackened with blood, sweat, and smoke. As he reached them he saluted them, "Helô Mam; Helô Tad."

"Morgan? What are you doing here?" asked Gwenllian.

"Helping farmers take back their lands of course," smiled Morgan, despite his parents' surprise and slight displeasure.

"How goes the battle, Morgan?" asked Gruffydd.

"There are few left alive of the Normans who came to confront us. Our leader in this glorious battle, Hywel ap Maredudd, Lord of Brycheiniog, is chasing Lord Maurice de Londres and his surviving followers back to Kidwelly Castle where they belong," reported Morgan proudly. "This land is free now; every farmer and shepherd displaced by the Normans can most certainly return to what is left of their homes and flocks. With your leave of course, f'arglwydd."

Gruffydd nudged his horse closer to his son and clapped him on the back, "Da iawn! Spread the word that I give my consent. The day is ours and to the people go the spoils of victory!"

January passed cold and dark. The snow fell heavily, trapping and killing many pregnant ewes and bringing great misery to Deheubarth. Embolden by their great victory at Carn Goch in the battle that came to be known as the "Battle of Llwchwr," people far and wide and from all corners of Deheubarth prepared for war. In Dinefwr Prince Gruffydd prepared for a long journey north through Norman-controlled Ceredigion to Gwenllian's home in Aberffraw.

"Take me with you, Gruffydd!" begged Gwenllian as Gruffydd sorted through the clothes he wished to bring with him.

"I need you here, Gwenllian. Who else will attend to the day to day government of our people?"

"Let Morgan or Maelgwn or even Owain handle that. They are certainly old enough to wield real power now!"

Gruffydd stopped and faced his wife, "I do not doubt that, Gwenllian."

"Then why? Why must you go and I stay? Why must I be parted from the love of my life and soul of my soul? Don't you know I cannot live without you?"

Gruffydd sighed, his wife's passionate plea striking him in his very heart, "I cannot live without you either, sweetheart! Do not doubt my love for a moment, I beg you!"

"Then why?"

"You are the best archer in all of Wales, Gwenllian. You are in every way equal to your brothers. There is no one in Gwynedd or Deheubarth save myself or your brother Owain perhaps who can match you in battle. You've proven that time and time again, just as you've proven yourself moderate in temperament and wise in judgement. You are the perfect queen for our people.

"That is why I need you to stay here. The marcher lords are likely to learn of my absence and once they do I have little doubt they will attack Deheubarth on the assumption that she is defenceless without her sovereign prince. The Normans do not see women as capable of governing and even less capable of leading men into battle. They will attack us. When they do, I need my greatest warrior leading our people and showing them the wisdom of rule by women," smiled Gruffydd, his heart breaking with the thought of leaving Gwenllian behind.

"The Norman barons have chosen King Stephen over Empress Matilda, haven't they?"

"By all reports, yes. Stephen will hold his first royal court on Easter Sunday in Westminster," confirmed Gruffydd.

"They will follow him in a war of conquest against us?"

"No one knows—but if they do, if this Stephen wants to conquer us then we must coordinate our efforts. It is not enough to affirm the friendship between Gwynedd and Deheubarth. To repel the full force of England's armies we must work together as one nation, one people."

Gwenllian fell into her husband's arms, "You really have to go without me, don't you?"

Gruffydd held her tightly, "I do not want to, my love! But yes, I am afraid I must."

"Deheubarth will be safe! If the English come, they will learn the folly of trespassing into our lands!"

"Of that, my dearest love, I have no doubt!"

Chapter Five

Two weeks after Prince Gruffydd ap Rhys' departure for Aberffraw a messenger arrived at Dinefwr castle, "F'arglwyddes I bring news!"

"What news?" asked Gwenllian.

"Norman ships have set sail from England with soldiers for Kidwelly Castle. The barons are giving Maurice de Londres thousands of fresh men. They say Maurice plans on avenging his losses at Carn Goch and slaughter every one, man or beast, who dares get in his way!"

"And King Stephen supports this?"

"Stephen is the crowned king of England but they say in practice the rule of the country is entirely in the hands of his barons. His barons want us all dead and our people enslaved, f'arglwyddes."

"How inconvenient to these Normans and their English subjects that we Cymraeg do not willingly give up our lands and flocks, that we possess the insolence to fight for what is ours."

"There is one more thing, f'arglwyddes. This Maurice de Londres does not uphold the code of chivalry. He does not fight by the rules."

Gwenllian picked up her bow, "Well then neither shall I. We shall meet his forces and defeat them. Sound the alarm. Let every able man and woman rise to our defence. We will stop Maurice de Londres once and for all!"

One week later Princess Gwenllian inspected her forces. In all of Deheubarth only two to three hundred men and women were strong enough to answer her call the arms. The rest of her people were too weak from the bitter winter and the recent famine created by the Normans to be able to assist her. Among those before her, most were farmers and shepherds armed only with the most simple of weapons and no armour to speak of. A few had shields, but not all of them. Only her sons Morgan and Maelgwn possessed formal training in warfare.

Convinced a direct confrontation would spell certain death for everyone, Gwenllian divided her forces. Half of her forces would stay with her in the woods just north of Kidwelly Castle to attack the Norman supply line. The other half would ride south to stop the Normans from leaving their ships. This second force she put in the hands of Gruffydd ap Llewelyn, a Welsh chieftain and one of her vassals, a man she believed to be honourable.

Two nights later Gruffydd ap Llewelyn slipped quietly out of the shadows. "Halt!" cried the knight watching over Maurice de Londres' encampment.

Gruffydd stepped closer to the knight, "I am here to see your master."

"Gruffydd?" asked the knight, recognizing him at last.

"Yes. It's me."

"You were gone for so long we were certain Prince Gruffydd and Princess Gwenllian had discovered you."

"Prince Gruffydd ap Rhys is in Aberffraw where he can do us no harm. The princess is alone and guarded only by her sons Morgan and Maelgwn."

"Glad tidings, indeed," smiled the knight as he escorted Gruffydd ap Llewelyn to his master.

As Gruffydd entered his pavilion, Maurice de Londres rose to meet him, "Any difficulties reaching us? Were you discovered?"

"No; no one knows I am here."

"Excellent news. What information do you have for me?"

"Half of the princess' solders are with me—poorly armed farmers you displaced this autumn. They have no training and will be very easy to dispatch as quickly or slowly as you wish," reported Gruffydd.

"And the rest?" asked Maurice.

"Gwenllian and her remaining men and women are hidden in the forest just north of Kidwelly Castle. The only properly armed and trained men at her disposal are her sons Morgan and Maelgwn. They are noble warriors and nearly as good with a bow as their mother."

"Yes. Gwenllian is a formable archer. We must make sure she cannot use those skills without an equal chance of hitting her own people. She's a woman and a one of some piety too. She won't kill unless she has to and never an innocent, no matter the cost. This is her weakness and one I am wholly without."

"As long as we are victorious, I do not care who you must kill or how many. I want the spoils you promised me!"

"Gladly," agreed Maurice.

The next morning Gruffydd ap Llewelyn rode in front of his army, "Good people of Deheubarth I am pleased to announce we will not be fighting the Normans today as they leave their ships. We have new orders, orders that will guarantee you warm beds and fully stomachs." Pausing dramatically Gruffydd watched as the people fell into confusion. "Nay, instead we are marching back north to Kidwelly Castle. The Normans will fight with us and not against us for we are allies fighting against the despotism of Princess Gwenllian who dares call herself equal to the men of Deheubarth. She does not want our freedom! She wants us under the yoke of Gwynedd, to be ruled by her father and her brothers. She is a serpent as vile as her sister-in-law Nest who preferred the bed of the English king and his dogs to that of a Welshman! I renounce Gwynedd. I renounce the tyranny of Gruffydd ap Rhys and his kin. No more! The Normans are our friends, not these traitors!"

Uncertain what to do and with few of them acquainted with anyone who knew their prince and princess personally, the people followed without question. An hour later the Normans joined them for the short march and the battle waiting for them.

As the sun reached its zenith overhead, the Normans led by Maurice de Londres and the Welsh led by Gruffydd ap Llewelyn spotted Gwenllian and her fighters encamped exactly where Gruffydd said they would be. Most were dining on their noon time meal, disarmed and relaxed despite the February chill. Quietly the well trained and well-armed Norman soldiers surrounded Princess Gwenllian's entire camp and closed in.

Suddenly a guard spotted the Normans and fired an arrow. Gwenllian heard the commotion and strung her bow. Morgan and Maelgwn spread through the ranks to sound the alarm and prepare for battle. As the Normans closed in, Princess Gwenllian fired at the Normans before mounting her horse and charging out of the forest into the open field that lay between them and the castle itself. Eager to escape the Norman infantry and knights, her people fled into the open ground.

As the Normans drove more and more Welsh out of the protection of the trees, Maurice de Londres sprung his trap. A massive force of one to two thousand swarmed out of the castle, pinning Gwenllian's defenders between the hammer and the anvil of his well-armed and well trained warriors. Pushed to the centre of the field Gwenllian dropped her bow; the tangle of bodies desperately swinging their weapons at anything that moved near them was so chaotic it was utterly impossible for her to hit the enemy without hitting her own brave defenders. Drawing her sword she charged ahead, her sons Morgan and Maelgwn dispatching the enemy efficiently and effectively just feet away from her as she valiantly slaughtered a dozen men.

It was not enough. Desperately the remains of her defenders tried to flee. The Normans left none alive. As the sun waned into late afternoon Princess Gwenllian gasped in horror as a Norman impaled Morgan on his sword before finishing the job with a circling cutting blow to the neck. Maelgwn cried out for his brother. A knight broke apart Gwenllian's shield with his mace, breaking her arm. Maelgwn rushed to his mother, blocking with his sword the blow meant to kill her and suffering great injury in the process.

Finally only Princess Gwenllian and Prince Maelgwn remained among the living. Maurice de Londres strutted before them imperiously as his soldiers tied her wrists together behind her back, "So we meet at last, princess!"

"You are Maurice de Londres I presume?"

Maurice laughed at her, "How could you guess?"

"Your reputation precedes you."

"You are the bane of this country, princess, a disease. I will cure our people of that disease."

"Our people, my lord? You are not of this country. You are a blood-thirsty Norman tyrant who feels the law of the sword is the way of righteousness! You who are quick to maim or kill over the slightest offences against the whims of your leaders! The people know who you are! They shall not forget what you do this day!"

"Enough! It is time for you and your son to die!" hissed Maurice. Quickly his men brought out a log from the castle. Kicking the princess and forcing Maelgwn to watch, he forced her down on her knees. Maurice held Gwenllian down upon the log face down as one of his knights drew his sword down hard upon her neck. Her head severed he pushed Maelgwn onto the bloodied log and dispatched him.

The Norman soldiers cheered as the heads of mother and son were held up for all to see, their blood lust quenched at last. Thirsty and jubilant the soldiers were delighted when Maurice brought out caskets of ale and mead for all to consume without restraint, many of them laughing at the sight of the princess' displayed head. For such was the temperament of the Normans, despite their claims of piety and the many notable churches and abbeys they built.

News of Princess Gwenllian's valour and courage spread through Deheubarth and across all the Welsh kingdoms. In Aberffraw Prince Gruffydd ap Rhys received the news like an arrow to his heart. Circled by the love and friendship of Gwenllian's family the prince resolved himself to avenging her dishonourable and murderous execution. Across every opportunity Prince Gruffydd ap Rhys and Gwenllian's brothers fought together to drive the Normans and the English out of Wales, winning many victories, including their great victory at Crug Mawr just north of Ceredigion in October. It was to be Prince Gruffydd ap Rhys' last victory. For early in eleven thirty seven both he and Gwenllian's father King Gruffydd ap Cynan followed her in death.

Years passed in constant warfare with the English. In time Gwenllian's brother Owain Gwynedd became king after their father. In Deheubarth younger son Rhys ap Gruffydd became Gwenllian's greatest legacy. For from his bloodline flowed the great hope for Wales when Owain ap Maredudd ap Tudur was born in Ynys Môn. And though the castle where Princess Gwenllian was born did not survive to Owain's time her life was still remembered in Gwynedd, in Deheubarth, and across all of Wales. As Owain helped King Henry the Fifth win against French at the Battle of Agincourt and as he secretly wed the dowager queen Catherine de Valois years later, the story of his foremother Princess Gwenllian ferch Gruffydd stayed ever dear to his heart.

Did his grandson, Henry Tudor remember the valour of Princess Gwenllian as he killed King Richard III in fourteen eighty five at the Battle of Bosworth Field? Who is to say?

The world is a strange place and history has a funny way of making right the evil deeds done against the innocent. And so one must think that surely in some place beyond this physical world, Princess Gwenllian ferch Gruffydd, the warrior princess of Deheubarth watched the coronation of Queen Elizabeth Tudor, a woman born of her blood and legacy, and smiled.

Timeline

844 Rhodri Mawr becomes king of Gwynedd

856 Rhodri Mawr defeats the Danes, protecting Gwynedd from Danish conquest.

871 Alfred the Great becomes King of Wessex and is declared king of England despite the limits to his actual power. Rhodri Mawr extends his realm into Carmarthenshire. Construction begins on Dinefwr castle soon after.

877 Death of Rhodri Mawr at the hands of Alfred the Great. Rhodri's sons Anarawd (King of Gwynedd and Powys) and Cadell (Seisyllwg) become vassals to King Alfred, beginning English claims over Welsh kingdoms.

886 Alfred the Great negotiates with the Danes, dividing the island into the Danelaw and giving Alfred the rest.

899 Death of King Alfred the Great of Wessex

900 Hywel ap Cadell ap Rhodri becomes king of Seisyllwg with Dinefwr Castle as his home and seat of power.

928 Hywel meets with leaders and scholars from across Wales and codifies the laws and customs of the Welsh peoples into one "Law of Wales."

930 Hywel founds the Kingdom of Deheubarth.

942 Hywel expands Deheubarth to include the kingdoms of Ceredigion, Powys, and Gwynedd. Over the next eight years Hywel consolidates most of Wales under his rule.

950 Death of Hywel. Wales breaks up into three major kingdoms: Deheubarth, Powys and Gwynedd, and Glamorgan. Deheubarth is ruled by three sons of Hywel: Owain, Rhodri, and Edwin.

953 Rhodri ap Hywel dies.

954 Edwin ap Hywel dies; Deheubarth is ruled entirely by Owain ap Hywel.

966 Birth of Æthelred II (the Unready) in England.

988 death of King Owain ap Hywel of Deheubarth. Owain's son Maredudd becomes king of Deheubarth.

1031 birth of Princess Ragnhildr to Olaf Sihtricson, king of Northumbria and Dublin and his wife, Princess Maelcorcre ingen Dúnlaing O'Muiredaig of Leinster.

1034 death of King Olaf Sihtricson. Prince Cynan ap Iago is born in Aberffraw, Ynys Môn.

1039 death of Iago ap Idwal, King of Gwynedd. Prince Cynan ap Iago flees to Ireland.

1055 Gruffydd ap Cynan is born in Dublin, Ireland to Irish Princess Ragnhildr and Prince Cynan ab Iago, a descendant of Rhodri Mawr.

1060 death of King Cynan ap Iago.

1063 Harold Godwinson leads an army into Wales, killing every adult Welshman in its path.

1063 5 August; Harold Earl of Wessex kills Gruffudd ap Llewelyn and marries his widow Ealdgyth. Harold Godwinson claims Wales as his kingdom in addition to his strong claim as heir to the weak and aging King Edward The Confessor of England. Wales breaks up into the principalities of Gwynedd, Powys, Gwent, Gwynllwg, Glamorgan, and Deheubarth. Deheubarth is taken over by Maredudd ap Rhydderch. King Harold gives control of Gwynedd to Bleddyn ap Cynfyn who rules it as king.

1065 birth of Angharad ferch Owain.

1066 5 January; death of King Edward the Confessor.

1066 6 January; Harold is crowned king of England in the palace of Westminster after the Witan meets and chooses him as king.

1066 7 January; Halley's Comet appears in the sky. The comet's appearance is regarded as an omen of doom for England.

1066 15 October; King Harold dies in the Battle of Hastings. Duke William of Normandy becomes King William I of England.

1067 Work begins on the first Norman castle in Wales in Chepstow.

1075 death of Anglo-Norman puppet King Bleddyn ap Cynfyn. Gruffydd ap Cynan claims the throne and attempts to free Gwynedd from Norman control. In defeat, Gruffydd flees to Ireland where he meets and marries Irish Princess Angharad ferch Owain.

1080 Princess Angharad gives birth to her son Owain, the future Owain Mawr and first to bear the title "Prince of Wales."

1081 Gruffydd ap Cynan bands with Prince Rhys ap Tewdwr of Deheubarth and successfully wins Gwynedd back from Norman control.

1082 King Gruffydd ap Cynan meets with Normans Hugh Earl of Chester and Hugh Earl of Shrewsbury. The meeting is a trap and King Gruffydd is imprisoned in Chester castle for many years. Earl Hugh and Robert of Rhuddlan take possession of Gwynedd and build the Norman castles at Bangor, Caernarfon and Aberlleiniog.

1084-1086 birth of Gruffudd ap Rhys ap Tewdwr, "the homeless prince" and his sister Princess Nest.

1093 Rhys ap Tewder king of Deheubarth perishes in Brycheiniog while assisting an ally resist conquest by Norman knights. King William Rufus of England sends in Norman barons to secure Deheubarth for England. Rhys' four surviving sons, including Gruffudd, temporarily escape into exile. Construction begins on Pembroke Castle

1094 King Gruffydd ap Cynan returns to Wales to lead a revolt against Norman fortifications across Gwynedd. The revolt spreads widely.

1095 - 1097 King William Rufus of England responds to King Gruffydd's revolt by sending in a series of largely unsuccessful assaults against Gwynedd that periodically force King Gruffydd ap Cynan to retreat to Ynys Môn and Ireland.

1097 birth of Gwenllian in Aberffraw, Ynys Môn to her father Gruffudd ap Cynan, King of Gwynedd, and his wife Angharad.

1099 Princess Nest becomes lover to Prince Henry of England.

1100 2 August King William Rufus dies in a hunting accident. His younger brother Henry ascends the throne of England as King Henry I.

1102 Gronwy ap Rhys is captured and dies in prison.

1103 Princess Nest gives birth to King Henry's bastard son Henry Fitzhenry. Henry marries Princess Nest off to Gerald de Windsor the constable of Pembroke Castle in charge of Norman controlled southern Wales.

1107; King Henry I establishes an English-Flemish colony in Haverfordwest in Pembrokeshire. English words begin to enter the Welsh language. Beginning of English attacks on Welsh language and culture, a cultural and linguistic war that endures until the 1999 formation of the Welsh Assembly in Cardiff.

1113; Gwenllian meets Prince Gruffydd of Deheubarth when he comes with his brother Hywel to Ynys Môn to meet with her father Gruffudd ap Cynan, Lord of Anglesey. Prince Gruffydd and Gwenllian quickly fall in love.

1114; King Henry I invades Gwynedd and forces King Gruffydd ap Cynan to swear fealty to him.

1115; Gruffydd ap Rhys and Gwenllian marry. Gwenllian moves to Dinefwr Castle in Deheubarth.

1116; Princess Gwenllian gives birth to her eldest son, Morgan ap Gruffydd.

1118; King Gruffydd ap Cynan delegates defence of Gwynedd to his sons Cadwallon, Owain Gwynedd and Cadwaladr. The brothers expand Gwynedd south and eastward.

1119; Princess Gwenllian gives birth to her second son, Maelgwn ap Gruffydd.

1126; Princess Gwenllian gives birth to her third son, Owain ap Gruffydd.

1128; Princess Gwenllian gives birth to her son Maredudd ap Gruffydd ap Rhys.

1129; Princess Gwenllian gives birth to Rhys "Fychan" ap Gruffydd, also known as Yr Arglwydd Rhys (The Lord Rhys), forefather of Owain ap Tudur and the Tudor Dynasty of England.

1130; Gwenllian gives birth to twin daughters Nest ferch Gruffydd and Gwladus ferch Gruffydd.

1132 Prince Cadwallon ap Gruffydd ap Cynan falls in battle against the kingdom of Powys near Llangollen.

1135 death of King Henry I of England. Henry's only surviving child Matilda claims the throne as queen regnant. A few weeks later his former lover Princess Nest dies in Wales.

1136 1st January; the battle of Llwchwr. Prince Gruffydd ap Rhys leaves for Aberffraw to meet with Owain and Cadwaladr ap Gruffydd concerning the best way to drive the Normans completely out of Wales.

1136 February; Maurice de Londres attacks Deheubarth. Princess Gwenllian leads her defensive forces and is captured near Kidwelly Castle before being publicly executed on Maurice's orders in a nearby field. Prince Maelgwn falls in battle trying to protect his mother from capture.

1136 29th March (Easter Sunday); King Stephen of England holds his first royal court in Westminster.

1136 15th April; the ambush slaying of the hated marcher lord Richard Fitz Gilbert de Clare near Llanthony Abbey north of Abergavenny encourages Deheubarth and Gwynedd to renew efforts to free Wales from Anglo-Norman control.

1136 October; Owain and Cadwaladr ap Gruffydd join with Prince Gruffydd ap Rhys of Deheubarth at the battle of Crug Mawr in Ceredigion, decidedly defeating the Normans.

1137 death of both Gwenllian's husband Prince Gruffudd ap Rhys ap Tewdwr and her father Gruffydd ap Cynan. Owain Mawr becomes king of Gwynedd and the first "prince of Wales."

1143 death of Anarawd ap Gruffydd, eldest son of Gruffydd ap Rhys.

1155 death of Prince Gruffydd and Princess Gwenllian's eldest son Maredudd.

1157 King Henry II invades Gwynedd.

1162 death of Queen Angharad ferch Owain of Gwynedd.

1170 28 November. Death of Owain Mawr.

1175 death of Cadell ap Gruffydd ap Rhys

1197 28 April; death of Princess Gwenllian's youngest son, Rhys ap Gruffydd ap Rhys.

1282 King Edward I of England conquers Wales. Deheubarth is broken up into three counties: Cardiganshire (Ceredigion), Carmarthenshire, and Pembrokeshire.

1282 December Llewelyn The Last, the last native prince of Wales, dies at the hands of Edward I's forces.

Suggest Reading and Bibliography

Gwenllian Ferch Gruffydd and Gruffydd ap Rhys

Wales – Land of my Fathers
http://waleslandofmyfathers.tumblr.com/post/55030484484/welsh-heroes-gwenllian-ferch-gruffydd-gwenllian

Stephen and the Welsh
http://history-england-the-anarchy.blogspot.com/2011/01/addendum-stephen-and-welsh.html

Did the Welsh Revolt of Gwenllian in 1136 contribute to the Evolution of the Arthurian Legend?
https://sites.google.com/site/arthurianmythandlegends/gwenllian-and-the-welsh-revolt-of-1136

Gruffydd ap Cynan, 1055-1037
http://www.englishmonarchs.co.uk/gruffydd_cynan.html

History Of Gruffudd Ap Cynan - A New Perspective
http://www.ancientwalesstudies.org/id46.html

Gwenllian
http://yba.llgc.org.uk/en/s-GWEN-FER-1100.html

Princess Nest
http://www.historic-uk.com/HistoryUK/HistoryofWales/Princess-Nest/

Owain Ap Cadwgan And Nest Ferch Rhys - An Historic Fiction?
http://www.ancientwalesstudies.org/id160.html
Owain Gwynedd
http://www.englishmonarchs.co.uk/owain_grufydd.html

Gruffudd Ap Rhys, The Homeless Prince
http://www.ancientwalesstudies.org/id197.html

Two Families Headed by Rhydderch ap Iestyn
http://www.ancientwalesstudies.org/id212.html

Gwenllian's Heritage and Legacy

Olaf Sihtricson of Dublin
http://www.mathematical.com/sihtricssonolaf2.html

Maelcorcre ingen Dúnlaing O'Muiredaig
http://www.mathematical.com/muirdagmaelcorce.html

Ragnhildr (Ragnaillt) verch Iago, Princess of Dublin (born Olaf), 1031 - 1076
https://www.myheritage.com/names/ragnhildr_olaf

Gwenllian
https://www.whobegatwhom.co.uk/ind3834.html

Rhys ap Gruffydd
http://www.castlewales.com/lrdrhys.html

Rhys "Fychan" ap Gruffydd, Prince of South Wales
http://www.mathematical.com/gruffuddrhys1127.html

The Children Of Lord Rhys
http://www.ancientwalesstudies.org/id187.html

The Dictionary of Welsh Biography: Gruffydd Ap Rhys
http://yba.llgc.org.uk/en/s-GRUF-APR-1090.html

The Dictionary of Welsh Biography: Anarawd ap Gruffydd
http://yba.llgc.org.uk/en/s-ANAR-APG-1143.html

The Dictionary of Welsh Biography: Cadell ap Gruffydd ap Rhys
http://yba.llgc.org.uk/en/s-CADE-APG-1175.html

The Dictionary of Welsh Biography: Maredudd ap Gruffydd ap Rhys
http://yba.llgc.org.uk/en/s-MARE-APG-1130.html

Anarawd ap Gruffydd
http://america.pink/anarawd-gruffydd_379512.html

Tywysog Cymru ac Arglwydd Eryri: Prince of Wales and Lord of Eryri
http://www.garthcelyn.org/#!the-princes/cfvg

Early Medieval Welsh History

Pais Dinogad
http://www.cs.ox.ac.uk/people/geraint.jones/rhydychen.org/about.welsh/pais-dinogad.html

The Oldest Welsh Lullaby: Dinogad's Smock (Pais Dinogad)
https://www.youtube.com/watch?v=ZBl7ZFI-QP8

St. David
http://www.britainexpress.com/wales/history/david.htm

BBC History: The Viking Challenge
http://www.bbc.co.uk/wales/history/sites/themes/periods/dark_ages04.shtml

When the Vikings Invaded North Wales
http://www.museumwales.ac.uk/articles/2007-04-02/When-the-Vikings-invaded-North-Wales/

Wales 550-800
http://www.britainexpress.com/wales/history/mercia-northumbria.htm

Gruffudd ap Llewelyn
http://www.britainexpress.com/wales/history/grufudd-ap-llewelyn.htm

Nest Ferch Cadell Ap Brochwel
http://www.ancientwalesstudies.org/id12.html

Rhodri Mawr
http://www.britainexpress.com/wales/history/rhodri.htm

Hywel the Good
http://www.britainexpress.com/wales/history/hywel.htm

The Celtic Literature Collective: The Laws of Hywel Dda
http://www.maryjones.us/ctexts/laws_hywel_dda.html

Medieval Laws of Hywel Dda published online by National Library of Wales
http://www.bbc.com/news/uk-wales-mid-wales-23579174

The Laws of Hywel Dda
http://www.bl.uk/onlinegallery/takingliberties/staritems/31lawsofhyweldda.html

Sara Woodbury: The Laws of Hywel Dda
http://www.sarahwoodbury.com/laws-of-hywel-dda/

Celtic Kingdoms of the British Isles: Deheubarth
http://www.historyfiles.co.uk/KingListsBritain/CymruDeheubarth.htm

The Battle of Llwchwr, 1Ionawr 1136
http://brwydr.blogspot.com/2007/05/battle-of-llwchwr-1-ionawr-1136.html

Early Medieval English History

Alfred The Great (871 – 899)
http://www.britroyals.com/kings.asp?id=alfred

BBC History: Alfred the Great
http://www.bbc.co.uk/history/historic_figures/alfred_the_great.shtml

English Monarchs: Sweyn
http://www.englishmonarchs.co.uk/vikings.htm

King Canute (1016-1035)
http://www.britroyals.com/kings.asp?id=canute

Brief History of the West Seaxe
http://www.twcenter.net/forums/showthread.php?142049-Faction-West-Seaxe-(Wessex)&s=b9488e25445a9e3e7156e0522464c764

The Norman Conquest

Harold of Wessex
http://www.historylearningsite.co.uk/medieval-england/harold-of-wessex/

The Norman Conquest
http://www.bbc.co.uk/wales/history/sites/themes/society/language_normans.shtml

The Norman Invasion of Wales
http://www.britainexpress.com/wales/history/marcher-lords.htm

The Norman and Angevin/Plantagenet kings of England, 1066-1377
http://hoocher.com/Henry_II_of_England/Norman_Plantagenet_Kings.gif

The descendants of Henry II and Eleanor of Aquitaine
http://historyofengland.typepad.com/.a/6a0147e0fd1b4a970b017744982c3b970d-pi

The Kings and Queens of England – Episode One Normans
https://youtu.be/0PfoYkgoBZQ

Norman Castles in Wales
http://www.castlewales.com/norman.html

Chepstow Castle
http://www.castlewales.com/chepstow.html

Pembroke Castle
http://pembroke-castle.co.uk/

BBC History: The Normans in Wales
http://www.bbc.co.uk/history/topics/normans_wales

The Normans
Part One – https://youtu.be/R7SX3ulV_tk
Part Two – https://youtu.be/aZ0Ny0jTiGc
Part Three – https://youtu.be/SSnXsYdJ9uo

Maps:

The Angevin "Empire"
http://www.heritage-history.com/maps/philips/phil035.jpg

Henry III's territories
http://www.heritage-history.com/maps/gardiner/gard012.jpg

Medieval England and Wales
http://www.heritage-history.com/maps/philips/phil034.jpg

Wales and the Marches in the Thirteenth Century
http://www.heritage-history.com/maps/philips/phil036c.jpg

Map of England by Matthew Paris
http://www.bl.uk/onlinegallery/takingliberties/images/319matthewparismapbig.jpg

Other Resources:

The History of the Welsh language
http://www.bbc.co.uk/cymru/cymraeg/yriaith/tudalen/welsh.shtml

How to Drink Like a Norman
http://blog.english-heritage.org.uk/how-to-drink-like-a-norman/

History of Europe
http://www.historyworld.net/wrldhis/PlainTextHistories.asp?ParagraphID=egw

The Saxons
http://www.ancient.eu/Saxons/

Places of Interest: Aberffraw
http://www.red-dragon-wales.com/PlacesofIntrest/Aberffraw.htm

Castles of the Welsh Princes
http://lostfort.blogspot.com/2010/10/castles-of-welsh-princes-rise-of-house.html

Celtic Kingdoms of the British Isles - Brycheiniog
http://www.historyfiles.co.uk/KingListsBritain/CymruBrycheiniog.htm

Williams, Patricia. *Historical Texts from Medieval Wales*. London: Modern Humanities Research Association, 2012.

About This Series

The Legendary Women of World History Series was first created in March 2014 in response to poor performance to a simple survey question asking people to name five women from across history whose lives still touch ours today. When less than 10% of the 50-100 people surveyed could name just five and less than 5% could name ten, author and historian Laurel A. Rockefeller decided to take action. The result was this author's best-selling narrative biography, "Boudicca, Britain's Queen of the Iceni" which came to audiences in audio edition in September of the same year.

In May 2015 work began on adapting the Legendary Women of World History Series into a stage drama series. The goal of the Legendary Women of World History Drama Series is both educational and entertainment, bringing the compelling stories of inspiring women to audiences while simultaneously offering commanding lead roles to actresses and offering educational settings enhanced opportunities working with the challenges of period dramas.

Today you can find the Legendary Women of World History Series and Legendary Women of World History Drama Series in English, French, Spanish, Chinese, Italian, Portuguese, German, and Welsh with more languages being offered as series popularity grows. It is the goal of this series to improve global history literacy while inspiring women and men with a more accurate understanding of history. It is the hope of this author and historian that the stage dramas will also help address inequities in the entertainment industry which so far have offered limited opportunities for women, people of colour, and religious minorities.

Thank you for reading this narrative biography. It is my fondest wish you will explore more of the Legendary Women of World History and be inspired!

Printed in Great Britain
by Amazon